The Power of Dorothy!

Spiritually Speaking: Words of Power and Inspiration for Everyone!

ROBERT MARK TEMPLE

WestBow Press
A DIVISION OF THOMAS NELSON

Unless otherwise marked, all Scripture quotations are from the King James Version;
they may be paraphrased to a degree, and all EMPHASIS is added by this author.

Scripture quotations marked (AMP) are from *The Amplified Bible
(AMP)*, copyright © 1954, 1958, 1962, 1964, 1965, 1987 by The
Lockman Foundation. Used by permission. All rights reserved.

WestBow Press books may be ordered through booksellers or by contacting:

WestBow Press
A Division of Thomas Nelson
1663 Liberty Drive
Bloomington, IN 47403
www.westbowpress.com
1 (866) 928-1240

Because of the dynamic nature of the Internet, any web addresses or
links contained in this book may have changed since publication and
may no longer be valid. The views expressed in this work are solely those
of the author and do not necessarily reflect the views of the publisher,
and the publisher hereby disclaims any responsibility for them.

Any people depicted in stock imagery provided by Thinkstock are models,
and such images are being used for illustrative purposes only.
Certain stock imagery © Thinkstock.

ISBN: 978-1-4908-1720-0 (sc)
ISBN: 978-1-4908-1722-4 (hc)
ISBN: 978-1-4908-1721-7 (e)

Library of Congress Control Number: 2013921431

Printed in the United States of America.

WestBow Press rev. date: 11/21/2013

To our parents, Althea and William Temple and Maggie and Patrick Hicks, who gave us life, hope, and faith—and not only *taught* us the Word of God and the ways of God in their own unique ways, but *lived* it!

Contents

Foreword

Praise
for
The Power of Dorothy

It is my great honor and delight to have been given this opportunity to write a foreword to this insightful new book of compiled daily inspirations written by my beloved friend and brother, Robert Mark Temple.

I strongly recommend its reading to believers and nonbelievers alike for its user-friendly practicality and relevance. I assure you that you will find this easily relatable anthology theologically sound and refreshingly edifying to your spirit.

In these times of radical moral decline where absolute truth and biblical standards are held in contempt rather than adhered to and revered as the rule of life, we need so desperately to hear the instructive voice of God through committed servants such as Robert Mark Temple.

This book promises to do just that—allow you to hear the distinct voice of God through the deep wisdom He has housed in the life and ministry of this servant of God!

As you enjoy *The Power of Dorothy*, you will indeed find yourself likewise spiritually empowered to withstand the unknown challenges of life in these uncertain times, and you will find yourself thanking God with me for the literary gift of Robert Mark Temple, my brother in Him.

—Elder Leon E. Swanson, founder/ director of Bema Outreach Ministries, Inc., Upper Marlboro, MD

What an assignment Robert Mark Temple has! Through the Word of God he has an endless supply of "nuggets of encouragement." What a powerful "weapon of our warfare" we find through his spirituality and the Holy Scriptures.

We have known Robert and his wife, Sallie, for over fifteen years. He, along with my husband, Michael, and I, labored together as ministers of the gospel in our former church, which is where we all met and became close friends. Simply put, I can only state that over the years, I have seen evidence of Robert's love for God, his wife, family, and friends, always willing to be there for them and for anyone who needed help. Scripturally, he actively demonstrates his dedication to Jesus' instruction found in Mark 16:15, "Go ye into all the world, and preach the gospel to every creature" (the Great Commission). Through technology (his blog), through face-to-face encounters, and through this book, he is able to carry out this assignment. Living a Christ-centered life, he demonstrates his love for God through selfless dedication to sharing the Word of God, bringing the "light of Jesus through salvation" into the heart of the unsaved and encouragement to the weary saint. In reading this book, if you open your heart, you will gain hope, encouragement, joy, insight, and peace in God's Word. You will find yourself thanking God that He "called" one Robert Mark Temple, and thankful for his acceptance of this assignment. Enjoy and be blessed!

—Rev. Michael David Drake I, pastor

Rev. Joyce Anita Drake

Rock of My Salvation Christian Church Ministries, Carmel, Indiana

Acknowledgments

Many thanks and love to my wife, Sallie; my children Maria and Christa; and my grandchildren Justin and Avionna (and another who is on her way from heaven).

Thanks to my entire family and friends of this ministry who have all given me the inspiration and support to accomplish one of my goals in life.

A Note from Robert

The title of this book came to me as I meditated and prayed about the type of people I wanted to reach. Throughout my life and ministry, the Lord has always encouraged and led me to speak from my heart, so that all people can gain understanding and insight into the wonderful knowledge of God's love through Jesus Christ.

As you read through the chapters of this book, it is my prayer that you will see that many of the challenges of Dorothy in the story of *The Wizard of Oz* mirror the challenges you face in this life.

Godspeed,
Robert

CHAPTER 1

The Power
of Dorothy

SCRIPTURALLY SPEAKING

"Finally, my brethren, be strong in the Lord and in the power of His might." (Ephesians 6:10)

SPIRITUALLY SPEAKING

What's the definition of power? Strength; ability (natural or moral); potent; possessing or exerting with great force; an inward God-given gift.

Jesus said in John 10:18, "No man taketh it from Me, but I lay it down of Myself. I have *power* to lay it down, and I have *power* to take it again. This commandment have I received of My Father."

Now that, my friends, is *power!*

Luke 15 tells the story of the Prodigal Son. When he returned home from the wild, living and having to eat hog slop in order to survive after his fortune ran out, his father was delighted and had a big party for him. But his older brother was not happy about it and would not join in. He complained to his father that he was the faithful son, yet no party was ever thrown for him.

I believe that's where many of us Christians find ourselves today. We constantly see sinners having big, fancy parties; living in big, fancy houses; driving expensive cars; having many of the finer things in life the average person may not ever see while working hard every day and obeying God's commandments! Sound familiar?

But even though the older son had permission, authority, and the power to have a party (enjoy the abundant life his father prepared for him), he didn't realize he could use it.

Many Christians today, much like the older son, find themselves living a life without the benefit of using the power they already possess.

At the end of the story in *The Wizard of Oz*, we find out that Dorothy had the power to go to her happy destination all the time! She just didn't know how to use it.

After the Resurrection, the following happened. "And Jesus came and spoke unto them, saying, *All power* is given unto me in heaven and in earth" (Matthew 28:18).

Friends, in order for us to effectively use the power that Jesus died to give us and live a victorious, abundant life, we must first be plugged into the Power Source. This comes by receiving Jesus as our personal Lord and Savior (being born again) and then being baptized in water and of the Spirit.

When Dorothy found herself in the Land of Oz, she followed the instructions of the Good Witch, used the power she already possessed, and found her way home.

Likewise, Christians who find ourselves in a world of sin and hypocrisy, like Dorothy, can exercise the power we already possess by following the instructions and commandments of the Good Shepherd!

Strangely, we can learn a lot from a fairy tale, can't we?

Let us always remember to do something that makes God smile today!

PRAYERFULLY SPEAKING

Father, I thank You for another day You have blessed me with to live here on earth. I thank You for Your grace and tender mercies. Help me, dear Lord, to use the power you died for, so I can defeat the enemy and live the abundant life. In Jesus' mighty and powerful name I pray, amen!

CHAPTER 2

The Power of Humility

SCRIPTURALLY SPEAKING

"Humble yourselves therefore under the mighty hand of God, that He may exalt you in due time." (1 Peter 5:6)

SPIRITUALLY SPEAKING

What's the definition of humility? Freedom from pride and arrogance; a modest estimation of your own worth; the ability not to think more highly of yourself than you ought to; not thinking that you are better than anyone else, but knowing that anything you have gotten, especially talent or promotion, is from God.

The Word of God says that the more talent and success we have, the more humble we should become. Some may think that this sounds a lot like weakness. Let's see what Jesus says about it in the gospel of Matthew.

In the following Scriptures, Jesus gives further insight about His Humility and Power. Matthew 11:28–30 (AMP) says,

> Come to me, all you who labor and are heavy-laden and over-burdened, and I will cause you to rest. [I will ease and relieve and refresh your souls.] Take My yoke upon you and learn of Me, for I am gentle (meek) and humble (lowly) in heart, and you will find rest (relief and ease and refreshment and recreation and blessed quiet) for your souls. For My yoke is wholesome (useful, good—not harsh, hard, sharp, or pressing, but comfortable, gracious, and pleasant), and My burden is light and easy to be borne.

Friends, it takes power to drop our human pride as Jesus did when He allowed John (the Baptist) to submerge Him in water. It established Him as being obedient to His Father, who then proclaimed to the world that Jesus was indeed His Son and that He was well pleased! What does that say about the power of humility?

Let's look at another example of what Jesus says about the power of humility in Matthew 23:11–12 (AMP): "He who is greatest among you shall be your servant. Whoever exalts himself [with haughtiness and empty pride] shall be humbled (brought low), and whoever humbles himself [whoever has a modest opinion of himself and behaves accordingly] shall be raised to honor."

In conclusion, here's what the Bible describes as humble: gentle, meek, lowly in heart, wholesome, useful, good, comfortable, gracious, pleasant, and refreshing.

Here's what humility is not: prideful, arrogant, immodest, thinking more highly of ourselves than we ought to, harsh, hard, sharp, exalting of self, and haughty.

I'd rather be humble (take on humility), love to serve others, and let God exalt me in due time than to exalt myself to the point where God lets my stubborn pride bring me down.

What about you?

Let us always remember to do something that makes God smile today!

PRAYERFULLY SPEAKING

Father, I thank You that this is another day You have blessed me to be here on earth. I thank You for Your grace and tender mercies and for demonstrating Your humbleness as an example for me. Father, I ask that You keep me humble under Your mighty hand, so that I may be exalted in due season. In Jesus' Mighty and Powerful Name I pray, amen!

CHAPTER 3

The Rewards
of Obedience

SCRIPTURALLY SPEAKING

"If you shall confess with your mouth the Lord Jesus, and shall believe in your heart that God has raised Him from the dead, you shall be saved." (Romans 10:9)

SPIRITUALLY SPEAKING

"Robert, if you don't do your chores right now …" Again, I'm remembering something my parents used to say when I was a boy. Isn't it strange how when we become adults, parents, aunts, or uncles, we begin remembering all the things our parents told us, especially when it comes to raising obedient children?

The definition of *obedience* is "compliance with a command" or "submission to authority."

My parents used different tactics, including raising their voice or the threat of using a belt, to get us to obey. We were usually pretty good about obeying our parents and teachers until a friend suggested we do something that we knew was against our parents' will. Punishment soon came when our parents found out about it.

When we look at the story of Adam and Eve, we see much the same thing. God gave Adam a specific set of instructions to obey in the Garden of Eden: "And the Lord God commanded the man, saying, You may freely eat of every tree of the garden; but of the tree of the knowledge of good and evil and blessing and calamity you shall not eat, for in the day that you eat of it you shall surely die" (Genesis 2:16–17 AMP).

Everything was going fine until the serpent tricked Eve into obeying him instead of God, and Adam followed suit. When

God found out that they had disobeyed Him, punishment soon followed.

In our focus Scripture we see what confessing in Jesus and believing that God raised Him from the dead gives us. "For as by one man's disobedience many were made sinners, so by the obedience of one shall many be made righteous" (Romans 5:19).

Salvation and everlasting life, a life full of joy and peace, come from obedience to the Word of God. What a reward that is!

Let us always remember to do something that makes God smile today!

PRAYERFULLY SPEAKING

Father, I thank You for another day You have blessed me to live here on earth. I thank You for Your grace and tender mercies. Help me, dear Lord, to obey Your Word so I can receive the rewards of salvation and live an abundant life full of joy, peace, and happiness. In Jesus' mighty and powerful name I pray, amen!

CHAPTER 4

Beauty for

Ashes

SCRIPTURALLY SPEAKING

"To appoint unto them that mourn in Zion, to give unto them *beauty* for *ashes,* the oil of joy for mourning, the garment of praise for the spirit of heaviness; that they might be called trees of righteousness, the planting of the Lord, that He might be glorified." (Isaiah 61:3)

SPIRITUALLY SPEAKING

Question: *Beauty for ashes?* What in the world are you talking about, Robert? Do you mean that God will give me beauty (something good, something of worth) for a bucket of ashes (something worthless)? Can you please explain to me why God would do this? It just doesn't make any sense to me!

Answer: Okay, my friend, I'll do my best.

Just recently while having a talk with a dear friend of mine, I found myself opening up my heart to him as to what was going on in my life and ministry. I explained to him that lately things hadn't gone as well as I expected or anticipated.

Some would say that my dreams of one day being a pastor of a successful, good-sized church had nearly gone up in flames! Later I realized that this represented my bucket of ashes. My friend, being a strong man of God, felt the Holy Spirit urge him to ask me to bring the Sunday morning message at his church—on Easter/Resurrection Sunday, no less! I was flabbergasted, to put it mildly. Later I realized that this represented God's way of giving me something of beauty for my ashes.

In the Old Testament book of the prophet Isaiah, chapter 61, verses 1 and 2, it speaks about the prophecy of Jesus when He declared His qualifications to preach the gospel (good news) to the meek, the poor, the afflicted, and the brokenhearted—to proclaim the year of His favor, the vengeance of God, and the comforting of people who mourn.

Verse 3 continues to focus on people who mourn. People mourn for different reasons: loved ones who have passed on, broken relationships, the loss of employment, financial issues, and, as in my case, the apparent loss of a dream.

But God, being the all-loving, all-caring God that He is, does not and will not ever leave us in the state of sadness or mourning for very long. That's why every Christian needs to have good, godly friends; good, godly counsel; one or more people they can talk with, exchange ideas with, offer good suggestions to, and cheer up when things go wrong—people who have a sincere heart for God.

Friends, I've experienced times when God uses people—men and women, boys and girls—to help deliver the oil of joy for mourning, the garment of praise for the spirit of heaviness. Not just to make us feel better, but so our peace can be restored, our feet replanted on solid ground, and, most important, that God might be glorified! Amen?

How's that for a good, godly answer?

Let us always remember to do something that makes God smile today!

PRAYERFULLY SPEAKING

Father, I thank You that this is another day You have blessed me to be here on earth. I thank You for Your grace and tender mercies and for demonstrating Your steadfast love for me. Father, I ask that You help me realize how much You love me and care for me, especially when I'm sad or in mourning. In Jesus' mighty and powerful name I pray, amen!

CHAPTER 5

Wow! Now That's Living!

SCRIPTURALLY SPEAKING

"For me to live is Christ [His life in me], and to die is gain [the gain of the glory of eternity]." (Philippians 1:21 AMP)

SPIRITUALLY SPEAKING

Do you *really* know that God loves you? Do I *really* know that God loves me? If we do, we can surely live a blessed life. If not, take heart because God does love you, and God does love me!

The abundant life is not just for some to live. It's available for all who believe in Jesus Christ; that He was born of the Virgin Mary, suffered under Pontius Pilate, was crucified, dead, and buried on Good Friday; was raised by God on the third day (Easter/ Resurrection Day); and now sits on the right hand of God the Father Almighty, making intercession for us, and later to judge the living and the dead! *Wow, now that's living!*

What can compare to the love of God? Nothing! What can separate us from the love of God? Nothing!

In our focus Scripture, the apostle Paul explains to the church in Rome that he is victorious in life and death because of Jesus! *Wow, now that's living!* Paul also does a unique dissertation in Romans, chapter 8: "No, in all these things we are more than conquerors through Him that loved us. For I am persuaded, that neither death, nor life, nor angels, nor principalities, nor powers, nor things present, nor things to come, nor height, nor depth, nor any other creature, shall be able to separate us from the love of God, which is in Christ Jesus our Lord" (Romans 8:37–39).

Friends, God loves us *so* much more than we can ever think or imagine! What a mighty God we serve! Now through the precious blood of Jesus, we have a responsibility to live so others will say, "Wow, now that's living!"

Let us always remember to do something that makes God smile today!

PRAYERFULLY SPEAKING

Father, I thank You for each and every day You have blessed me to be here on earth. I thank You for Your grace and tender mercies toward me. Father, I ask that You help me believe in my heart just how much You love me, for I am not worthy by myself, but through the precious blood of Jesus Christ I am made worthy. In Jesus' mighty and powerful name I pray, amen!

CHAPTER 6

Get Some Help!

SCRIPTURALLY SPEAKING

"Listen now to [me]; I will counsel you, and God will be with you. You shall represent the people before God, bringing their cases and causes to Him." (Exodus 18:19 AMP)

SPIRITUALLY SPEAKING

If you lead a busy life like I do, it's not very hard for some of us to characterize ourselves as overextended, right?

This is the situation where Moses found himself in the Old Testament book of Exodus, chapter 18. It continues the story of how the Lord helped Moses and the Israelites escape Pharaoh and the Egyptians.

Although the Israelites rejoiced, they encountered many hardships as they were living in the wilderness. They needed a lot of help from Moses, and he gave it to them from morning until evening.

When Jethro, Moses' father-in-law, saw that he was overextending himself, he knew it wasn't good for Moses. He knew he would soon wear himself out, so he advised Moses to get some help. Moses did just that.

What we can learn from this story is twofold. First, we must be willing to listen to good, godly counsel. Second, we must be willing to get some help if need be. Moses was successful because he chose to do both.

Friends, there was a time not long ago when I became overextended. I was proud of being "Mr. Multitask"! I was always busy at work; always busy doing church work; always helping out around the house; always helping friends, neighbors, and relatives; etc.

And while I sincerely enjoyed doing it all, if I had kept up that pace for too long, I would have surely wound up in the hospital from exhaustion or worse. Who would I be able to help then? But God, being the Wonderful Counselor that He is, sent some good, godly advisors and counselors my way who explained to me what Jethro said to Moses. Namely, *get some help!*

Ask for help. Delegate some of those tasks you do. Don't try to do everything yourself, or you'll wear yourself out or even worse!

If you can see yourself in this story (I'll bet more than a few of you will), take heed. It took being humble and dropping my stubborn pride in order to be willing to listen to good, godly counsel and choose to change my ways.

When Dorothy found herself in the Land of Oz needing help to find her way home, she found the Scarecrow, the Lion, and the Tin Man, each one offering her hope and a way out.

How about you? Is this the day you stop killing yourself as I almost did, trying to do it all? Trying to do it all at once without asking for help?

Deuteronomy 30:19 (AMP) sums it up this way: "I call heaven and earth to witness this day against you that I have set before you life and death, the blessings and the curses; therefore *choose life*, that you and your descendants may live."

Help me, dear Lord, to live!

PRAYERFULLY SPEAKING

Father, I thank You for each and every day You have blessed me to be here on earth. I thank You for Your grace and tender mercies toward me. Father, I ask that You help me ask for help when I need it, especially when I am trying to do too much by myself. In Jesus' mighty and powerful name I pray, amen!

CHAPTER 7

Be Still!

SCRIPTURALLY SPEAKING

"Be still, and know that I am God: I will be exalted among the heathen, I will be exalted in the earth." (Psalm 46:10)

SPIRITUALLY SPEAKING

"Will you pleeeeease be still?" I can still hear the voice of my parents sharing that phrase with me from time to time when I would not stop squirming for one reason or another. I'm betting some of you can too!

I'm also pretty sure that most teachers, aunts, uncles, cousins, and babysitters have also said the same thing from time to time.

I remember when my wife was having eye surgery some years ago. After it was a success, the surgeon shared with me that if she had not been completely still during the surgery, she might have lost the eye!

In today's focus Scripture, David is expressing God's majestic power on the earth. God needed His people to know that there are times when battles, wars, and certain situations are not ours to fight, but His. Instead, they call for us to take a "time-out," "be still," and wait for God's instructions before we move.

Friends, *being still* doesn't mean for us to wait around doing nothing, nor does it mean for us to stay in bed or in our easy chair all day either. We listen to the Word of the Lord for further instructions.

Let's look at what happened when the Spirit of the Lord God came upon Jahaziel, the son of Zechariah, when the inhabitants of Jerusalem squirmed upon looking at their adversaries who greatly outnumbered them: "He said, Hearken, all Judah, you inhabitants of Jerusalem, and you King Jehoshaphat. The Lord says this to you: Be not afraid or dismayed at this great multitude; for the battle is not yours, but God's" (2 Chronicles 20:15 AMP).

After they listened to God's instructions, let's see what happened to them next: "You shall not need to fight in this battle; take your positions, *stand still,* and see the deliverance of the Lord [Who is] with you, O Judah and Jerusalem. Fear not nor be dismayed. Tomorrow go out against them, for the Lord is with you" (2 Chronicles 20:17 AMP).

In other words, they wisely waited for God's specific instructions *before* they acted!

The following Scripture in the Word of God is also eye-opening: "Rest in the Lord, and wait patiently for Him: fret not thyself because of him [or her] that prospers in his [or her] way, because of the [one] who brings wicked devices to pass" (Psalm 37:7).

Be still, know that I am God, and rest! It looks to me like our parents were taking a page out of the Word of God when they said to us emphatically, "Will you pleeeeease be still!"

Sounds like mighty good advice to me!

Let us always remember to do something that makes God smile today!

PRAYERFULLY SPEAKING

Father, I thank You for another day You have blessed me with to live here on earth. I thank You for Your grace and tender mercies. Help me, dear Lord, to remember to be still, rest in You, and listen for instructions when situations in my life seem overwhelming. In Jesus' mighty and powerful name I pray, amen!

CHAPTER 8

Keeping Your Peace

SCRIPTURALLY SPEAKING

"The Lord will fight for you, and you shall hold your peace and remain at rest." (Exodus 14:14 AMP)

SPIRITUALLY SPEAKING

Friends, "Hold your peace," "Keep the peace," "Live in peace," "I'm at peace," "I come in peace," "Go in peace," and "Give peace a chance" are all different sayings, yet all have their root meaning based in the same word: *peace*, which is the opposite of confusion.

It was very early in my life when I learned that different people treated me differently. Although I tried to be friends with everyone, not everyone wanted to be friends with me.

For no apparent reason, some people always had critical and mean things to say to me, no matter how nice or good I was to them. Being a very shy and quiet individual back then, I didn't really say much, but each time I was attacked, it hurt.

Many times I wanted to fight back out of my anger but didn't (most of the time, that is). I continued to be hurt and abused. Because I took most of the insults to heart, there wasn't very much peace in my life at all.

Then I learned that peace is something the Word of God speaks about often. Jesus said in John 14:27, "Peace I leave with you, My peace I give to you: not as the world gives, (do I) give to you. Let not your heart be troubled, neither let it be afraid."

Friends, the Bible says that once we receive Jesus Christ into our hearts as our Lord and Savior, the peace of God becomes a part of us! We just need to practice and make a conscious decision to activate it and use it. The choice is ours.

When we use the peace of God in us to override the evil spirit in others determined to steal our peace, the devil, haters, mean-spirited people, and unbelievers are defeated, and the victory is ours to enjoy!

The moment we stop allowing ourselves to be agitated, disturbed, intimidated, fearful, or unsettled, we will discover the peace that God is working behind the scenes to accomplish, fighting our battles for us.

Let's always remember to do something that makes God smile today!

PRAYERFULLY SPEAKING

I thank You, dear Lord, for reminding me that You have given me Your peace and have promised to fight my battles for me if I just keep still. In Jesus' mighty and powerful name I pray, amen.

CHAPTER 9

The Search
for Peace

SCRIPTURALLY SPEAKING

"The *peace of God,* which passes all understanding, shall keep your hearts and minds through Christ Jesus." (Philippians 4:7)

SPIRITUALLY SPEAKING

Friends, I can remember one of my dad's favorite greetings when anyone would come to visit him: "How are you getting along?"

Although his question was general in nature, I really think he was trying to gauge if the person, usually a family member, was having a hard time or a good time. Were we dealing with strife, or were we at peace?

An often-asked question for many beauty pageant contestants is what they would work for if they won the contest. The answer is very often "World peace."

The search for peace continues in the world in which we live. Jesus said that there would be wars and rumors of wars (Matthew 24:6). But in your personal life, you may be wondering if you'll ever experience *real peace*, especially when strife seems to be all around you.

But rest assured that there is good news! Jesus lived, died, and lives again for us to have peace.

The Bible says in 1 Peter 5:7 (AMP), "Casting the whole of your care [all your anxieties, all your worries, all your concerns, once and for all] on Him, for He cares for you affectionately and cares about you watchfully."

You may be thinking, *I wish it were that easy.* But much like anything else in life, as the saying goes, "Practice makes perfect!"

The Word of God says in Philippians 2:3, "Let nothing be done through strife or vainglory [I know I'm right, so it must be someone else's fault]; but in lowliness of mind let each esteem others better than themselves."

There is no peace without depending on God to lead us and guide us, believing through prayer and faith that He indeed has all the answers. It's a heart thing. "Blessed are the pure in heart: for they shall see God" (Matthew 5:8).

We can indeed live a peaceful life. It begins with you; it begins with me.

Let's not forget to do something that makes God smile today!

PRAYERFULLY SPEAKING

I thank You, dear Lord, for reminding me that to enjoy and maintain peace in my life, I must believe and depend on You and Your Word. Help me, dear Lord, to strive to live at peace with everyone, starting with myself. In Jesus' mighty and powerful name I pray, amen!

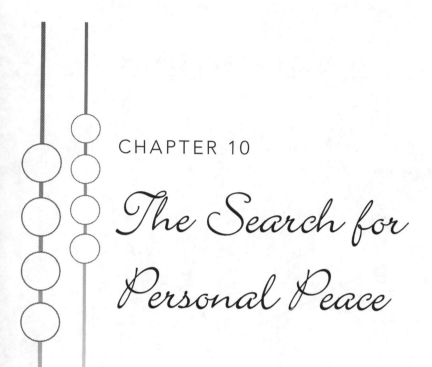

CHAPTER 10

The Search for Personal Peace

SCRIPTURALLY SPEAKING

"If it is possible, as far as it depends on you, *live at peace with everyone.*" (Romans 12:18 AMP)

SPIRITUALLY SPEAKING

Friends, I can remember back in the sixties, one of the most common greetings was to say, "Peace," to a friend. There were "peace marches" in Washington, DC; hippies were all about peace; there were bumper stickers and placards galore stating, "Peace, not war," and "Give peace a chance!"

Peace is the opposite of turmoil, and if we are going to live at peace with everyone, it starts within ourselves.

I am basically a very peaceful, laid-back individual. But when the winds of strife begin to blow in my life … not so much. Because I am a family man of God, a minister, and a professional manager, there are lots of people who depend on me and look to me to stay calm, cool, and collected, especially during a crisis.

The Word of God says in 1 Thessalonians 4:11a (AMP), "To make it your ambition and definitely endeavor to *live quietly and peacefully,* to mind your own affairs [business] …"

So if my personal life is in turmoil, I find that I have to work harder on myself to be effective as a leader and mentor. I am the first one who needs to be calm. It takes a *lot* of prayer, discipline, and willpower to be a good, peaceful example to my family, church members, and the people I interact with at work.

I can't wait until challenging things happen to begin to pray. The Bible says in 1 Thessalonians 5:17, "Pray without ceasing." In other words, we are to remain in a prayerful state at all times. To do this is to stay connected to the Power Source, the Holy Spirit of the living God! We must read and meditate on the Word of God on a regular and consistent basis. We simply must!

Jesus said an astounding thing in John 14:27 (AMP): "Peace I leave with you; *My [own] peace* I now give and bequeath to you. Not as the world gives do I give to you. (My peace is permanent). Do not let your hearts be troubled, neither let them be afraid. [Stop allowing yourselves to be agitated and disturbed; and do not permit yourselves to be fearful and intimidated and cowardly and unsettled.]"

Believe it or not, peace is a personal choice! How do you get there? When you become "born anew" in Jesus Christ, the power to be peaceful is already inside you!

God has already given it to us through Jesus Christ. It's up to us to learn to use it.

Let's remember to do something that makes God smile today!

PRAYERFULLY SPEAKING

I thank You, dear Lord, for reminding me that I must have peace inside myself in order to live peacefully with all people. Help me, dear Lord, to stay connected to the Holy Spirit, so I can access the power to do so. In Jesus' mighty and powerful name I pray, amen!

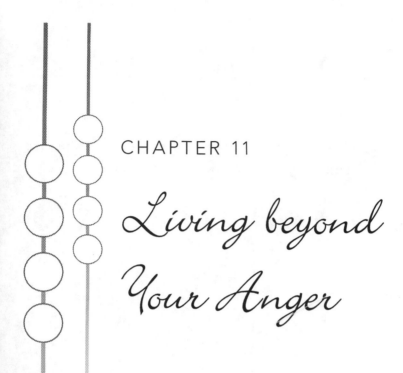

CHAPTER 11

Living beyond Your Anger

SCRIPTURALLY SPEAKING

"He who is *slow to anger* is better than the mighty, he who rules his (own) spirit [is better] than he who takes a city." (Proverbs 16:32 AMP)

SPIRITUALLY SPEAKING

Friends, some say that three of the most negative emotions are anger, guilt, and fear. Many agree that anger is number one.

It is also the strongest and most dangerous of all passions. Oftentimes when a crime is described as being one of passion, that means it was probably fueled by anger. Anger is such a dangerous emotion that it can lead to abuse, divorce, broken friendships or fellowships, prison time, and even death.

But what does the Word of God say about anger? Is all anger bad?

"When angry, do not sin; do not ever let your wrath (your exasperation, your fury, rage, or indignation) last until the sun goes down" (Ephesians 4:26 AMP). Be "slow to anger" (Proverbs 16:32). Be "ready to forgive" (Psalm 86:5).

In the Old Testament, Moses lost a privilege he had looked forward to for years (entering the Promised Land), due to uncontrolled anger (see Numbers 20:1–12).

However, many people involved in the civil rights movement in the 1950s and '60s, like the Rev. Dr. Martin Luther King Jr., had plenty of anger but made a conscious decision to use it righteously, nonviolently.

Consider this: Anger is *not* a sin. It is what we do with it that can become a sin. Anger cannot be expected to go away just because we are Christians. How we learn to manage it is what makes the difference.

One thing is for sure. If we don't deal with our anger quickly, we will eventually either explode or implode.

A good thing to do when we find ourselves angry is to stop and count to ten *before* we speak or respond. Some of us should probably count to a hundred or take a walk before responding. (Amen, Robert?)

I've found that the best way to deal with my anger is to take it to God in prayer. I've found that if I tell God all about it and then ask God to help me handle it, manage it in a godly way, He will. Many a mistake has been made because we don't take our angry thoughts to God first (James 4:2).

I've also learned that He may direct me to a mature friend or professional, someone who will listen with the love of God in his or her heart and give me godly advice. Many times it is good to wait for God's timing before responding to our anger. Timing can be crucial in determining a successful outcome or a conflict resolution.

Obeying and meditating on God's Word is good medicine for our souls and spirits. It not only brings instructions, but it comforts in every way.

Let's always remember to do something that makes God smile today!

PRAYERFULLY SPEAKING

I thank You, dear Lord, for reminding me to take everything, every problem, every angry thought I may have to You before I respond. I believe that You will give me the godly way to handle and manage them through Your precious Holy Spirit. In Jesus' mighty and powerful name I pray, amen!

CHAPTER 12

Armored, Armed, and Dangerous

SCRIPTURALLY SPEAKING

"Put on *God's whole armor,* [the armor of a heavy-armed soldier which *God* supplies], that you may be able successfully to stand up against [all] the strategies and deceits of the devil." (Ephesians 6:11 AMP)

SPIRITUALLY SPEAKING

Friends, a sure way to know that police are looking for someone who is a threat to society is to hear them say, "The suspect is *armed and dangerous.*"

While it may sound strange to some, as people of God and according to the Word of God, we are in a war (spiritual warfare) between the forces of evil and the kingdom of God!

"For we wrestle not against flesh and blood, but against principalities, against powers, against the rulers of the darkness of this world, [and] against spiritual wickedness in high places" (Ephesians 6:12).

But unlike many conflicts around the world today that are fought with deadly weapons, as Christians we are called to fight the good fight of faith by believing and using God's Word to fight our battles (see 1 Timothy 6:12).

In order to successfully defeat the enemy, we need to be armed with God's Word and considered dangerous to our enemies. "So be subject to God. Resist the devil [stand firm against him], and he will flee from you" (James 4:7 AMP).

If Jesus was strong enough to say to the devil, "Get thee behind me, Satan!" (Luke 4:8), then so are we.

Personally, I've got more than a few battle scars to prove that I am a "soldier in the army of the Lord." Though we may lose a battle here and there, the war is already won by the death, burial, and resurrection of Jesus Christ!

Though we may be injured because we live and fight our adversaries with our faith words, the Bible states that God has made a way for us to be restored to health and made whole, not remain full of holes. His name is Jesus!

"And wherever He [Jesus] entered, into villages or cities or the country, they would lay the sick in the marketplaces and beg Him that they might touch even the fringe of His outer garment: and as many as touched Him were restored to health" (Mark 6:56 AMP).

Three things have made true believers victorious today: the power of the Word of God, the power in the name of Jesus, and the power through the blood of Jesus.

Are you considered armed and dangerous to the enemies in your life because the Word of God lives inside you? Do demons flee when they see you coming?

Friends, to gain the victory in our everyday life and throughout our faith walk, we have to put our spiritual armor on, covering the crown of our head down to the soles of our feet, and walk in love and faith, praying always with all praying and supplication in the Spirit (Ephesians 6:13–18).

Let's always remember to do something that makes God smile today!

PRAYERFULLY SPEAKING

I thank You, dear Lord, for reminding me to keep my spiritual armor on by living in and by Your Word. In Jesus' mighty and powerful name I pray, amen!

CHAPTER 13

The War Within

SCRIPTURALLY SPEAKING

"For I do not understand my own actions [I am baffled, bewildered]. I do not practice or accomplish what I wish, but I do the very thing that I loathe [which my moral instinct condemns]." (Romans 7:15 AMP)

SPIRITUALLY SPEAKING

Friends, I don't know about you, but there are times in my life where my intention was to do the right thing, but my actions wound up being the opposite of what I had planned (the wrong thing).

Being led by the Spirit of God, I have attempted to edify someone or to make peace with a loved one, a coworker, or my wife and children. But soon, what came out of my mouth in no way matched what was in my heart and mind! What happened?

Was I letting my emotions get the best of me? Was I being too quick on the draw rather than being "slow to anger" (Psalm 103:8)?

The Bible says, "For we *wrestle* not against flesh and blood, but against principalities, against powers, against the rulers of the darkness of this world, against spiritual wickedness in high places" (Ephesians 6:12).

The Word of God teaches us that once we become "born again" (John 3:3; 1 Peter 1:23), we have the power not to willfully, habitually, or purposely sin, because the nature of God dwells within us. Although everyone sins—is guilty of wrongdoing (Romans 3:23)—for the true believer it becomes very uncomfortable doing so.

I've found that the best ways to fight enemy spirits are to pray regularly (for which there is no substitute); consistently meditate on God's holy Word (marinating in it); read the Word of God (and other godly books for my own understanding and edification); and consistent fellowship with other (true) believers (Proverbs 27:17).

Friends, "the war within us" is not an easy one to fight alone. We need help. And as our Lord and Savior Jesus Christ said in John 16:33, "These things have I spoken unto you, that in me you might have peace. In the world you shall have tribulation: *but be of good cheer; I have overcome the world.*"

That's good news! We can and we shall win the war within with the Holy Spirit of the Living God being our helper!

Let's always remember to do something that makes God smile today!

PRAYERFULLY SPEAKING

I thank You, dear Lord, for reminding me that I can indeed win the war within myself by believing and counting on You being my help. In Jesus' mighty and powerful name I pray, amen!

CHAPTER 14

Maggie's Mission of Love

SCRIPTURALLY SPEAKING

"I have fought a good fight, I have finished my course, I have kept the faith." (2 Timothy 4:7)

SPIRITUALLY SPEAKING

Friends, Sister Maggie Hicks, who peacefully passed away in her sleep on March 2, 2013, nine days short of her ninety-first birthday, was technically my mother-in-law. But in all actuality, she was a loving mother, not just to me but to virtually everyone she met.

A very popular name people called her, Mother Hicks, was not used just because she was a member of the Piney Grove Baptist Church Mothers' Board. She was indeed loved like a mother by everyone who came in contact with her.

Just as a United States soldier in Afghanistan or any other part of the world is on a mission to protect, Maggie Hicks was on a mission of love.

The essence of her smile brought love to its recipients in a special way, exceeded only by her kindnesses.

She was the definition of a Christian, not only because of her undying love for God, Jesus, and the Holy Spirit, but by virtue of her love and sacrifice for her late husband, Patrick Henry Hicks; her children, Patricia, Sallie, Eva Rebecca, Willie, Kathleen, Curtis, and Juanita; their spouses; her numerous grandchildren, great-grandchildren, nieces, and nephews ... the list goes on and on. She loved us all dearly, and we all loved her dearly! "God is love" (1 John 4:8).

There was absolutely no one she didn't love and try to help. She could be stern when she needed to be and faithful and steadfast, as when she taught Sunday school.

There was nothing she wouldn't do for you. All you had to do was ask, and sometimes you didn't even have to do that.

I'll never forget when my youngest daughter, Christa, was born and we took her to see Grandma Maggie. I just about fainted when *she asked me* if she could have a hand in raising her! I should have been the one asking her! Such humility was commonplace for her.

As David wrote in Psalm 23, which I had the honor and pleasure of reading at her glorious homegoing service, "The Lord is my shepherd; I shall not want."

The Lord was indeed her Shepherd. The Lord, as well as her children and loved ones, saw to it that she wanted for nothing in this world.

God gave her a peaceful way to live and such a peaceful way to go. "Well done, My Good and Faithful Servant. Well done! Enter into the joy of the Lord" (paraphrasing Matthew 25:23).

Mission of love accomplished!

Let's always remember to do something that makes God smile today (like living by love and faith in memory of one Maggie Hicks)!

CHAPTER 15

Time to Guard Your Heart

SCRIPTURALLY SPEAKING

"Keep [guard] your heart with all diligence; for out of it are the issues of life." (Proverbs 4:23)

SPIRITUALLY SPEAKING

Friends, there are times when you need to set boundaries around your heart to protect it from verbal abuse and harmful accusations.

Many times you can get deeply hurt by someone you don't know or even worse by someone close, someone near and dear to your heart.

More and more I've seen people hurt by an unexpected cruel comment, accusation, or unfounded judgment. It's usually a time when your guard is down and your heart is unprotected or vulnerable.

There are two kinds of boundaries: protective and containing. A protective boundary is an outer shell of insulation that will protect your heart from the cruelties of the world. Without it you are open to every attack and penetrating word someone may say.

A protective boundary serves as a wall with a gate. When statements of any kind are directed toward you, you can mentally stop them at the wall. Ask yourself this question *before* you open the gate to your heart: "Is this statement true or untrue?"

If it is not true, don't open the gate to the "soft spot" of your heart. If it is true or partly true, that's a time for reflection or possible ownership.

A containing boundary is like an inner filter that protects the world from our statements, verbal abuse, or harmful accusations. As a child of the most high God, I have no business opening my mouth to say anything I want, to whomever I want, anytime I want, anywhere I want. I need to stop and filter my thought pattern *before* I choose to speak.

The Word of God in Proverbs 4:24 (AMP) states, "Put away from you false and dishonest speech, and willful and contrary talk put *far* from you."

The guarding of our hearts will save us from heartbreak; the discipline of our speech will demonstrate the power of the Holy Spirit, which gives us self-control. When we pattern our behavior after the love of God, it is an example of positive expression and encouragement and keeps the heart of a true Christian healthy and joyful.

Let's always remember to do something that makes God smile today!

(A hearty thank-you to Ginger Sullivan's inspiration.)

PRAYERFULLY SPEAKING

I thank You, dear Lord, for reminding me of the importance of guarding my heart from unholy intrusions to stop the fiery darts of the wicked. I also thank You for giving me the power of Your Holy Spirit to help me filter my speech before I open my mouth. In Jesus' mighty and powerful name I pray, amen!

CHAPTER 16

Ready, Aim, Love!

SCRIPTURALLY SPEAKING

"For God so loved the world that He gave His only begotten Son, that whosoever believes in Him should not perish, but have everlasting life." (John 3:16)

SPIRITUALLY SPEAKING

Friends, many of us have heard the popular phrase, "Ready, aim, fire!" In my younger days, I can remember watching TV westerns that used that phrase in many episodes; usually when cowboys and Indians fought.

Today, that phrase is unpopular due to the outrageous amount of violence not only in other places around the world but here in America.

Sometimes I ask myself, *What happened? Why is there so much hatred? Why is there so much "man's inhumanity to man"?* as Rev. Dr. Martin Luther King Jr. said at the height of the civil rights movement.

Where's the love that God gave to us through many of His people and prophets over thousands of years? Where's the sacrificial love that our Lord and Savior Jesus Christ lived and died for (and lives to pour out again through the Holy Spirit)?

It seems as though hatred and killing have somehow replaced love, sacrifice, giving, and forgiving! Isn't love supposed to conquer all (1 Corinthians 13:8)?

If I had one wish for the world today, it would go like this: "Love endures long and is patient and kind; love never is envious nor boils over with jealousy, is not boastful or vainglorious, does not display itself haughtily. ... *love never fails*" (1 Corinthians 13:4, 8 AMP).

"And so faith, hope, love abide [*faith*—conviction and belief respecting man's relation to God and divine things; *hope*—joyful and confident expectation of eternal salvation; *love*—true affection for God and man, growing out of God's love for and in us], these three; *but the greatest of these is love*" (1 Corinthians 13:13 AMP).

Friends, God's unconditional love is so much better, much more powerful than hatred. Let's get ready to aim for love instead of hate! Amen? Amen!

Let us always remember to do something that makes God smile today!

PRAYERFULLY SPEAKING

I thank You, dear Lord, for reminding me to always be ready to love like You because You are love, and You gave me Your best by giving me Jesus as a sacrifice for my sins. In Jesus' mighty and powerful name I pray, amen!

CHAPTER 17

Invitation to

Salvation

If you haven't accepted Jesus Christ as your personal Lord and Savior, why not do it today? It's easier than you think. Just say with a sincere heart, "Lord Jesus, I believe in my heart, and confess with my mouth, that You are Lord. I submit my life to You as my Lord and Savior.

"I believe You died for me to wash away all my sins. I ask You to forgive me of my sins as I forgive others, and come into my heart so I might live a brand-new life. In Jesus' name I pray, amen!"

That's it! Heaven is rejoicing! Welcome to the body of Christ!

About the Author

Robert Mark Temple was born and raised in St. Louis, Missouri. He was educated in St. Louis public schools and attended St. Louis University where he studied sociology, world religion, and business administration.

From his childhood he was an active member of the St. Peter's AME Church. He felt the call to preach at age twenty-six while teaching a Sunday school class based on Joshua 24:15, "As for me and my house, we will serve the Lord." He was first licensed to preach the good news of the gospel of Jesus Christ while a member of the Coleman Temple CME Church. While studying "The Living Word" classes at St. Louis Bible Way Church, he became born again and baptized in the Holy Spirit.

After moving to the Washington, DC, area in 1984, he studied ministry at Howard University Divinity School. In August 2006 after serving on several church ministerial staffs, he felt "the clarion call of God" to be founder and pastor of Word of God Gospel Fellowship Church, Inc., in suburban Maryland. He was officially ordained and installed as pastor in September 2011 by Rev. Michael David Drake I, pastor of Rock of My Salvation Christian Church Ministries, Inc., Carmel, Indiana.

He has been writing a series of daily inspirational messages called "The Word for Today" since October 2011, which is now produced in blog form.

He has been happily married to Sallie Elizabeth Temple since 1986, and has two lovely daughters, Maria and Christa, and two wonderful grandchildren, Justin and Avionna, and another one on the way.

He believes in the Lord Jesus Christ as his Savior and credits his wife and family as his anchors. His vision for the church is that the body of Christ would truly walk in the love of God and His Word (John 3:16) and live the "abundant life" Jesus spoke of in John 10:10 (AMP): "The thief comes only in order to steal and kill and destroy. I came that they may have and enjoy life, and have it in abundance (to the full, till it overflows)."

www.WordofGodGospelFellowshipChurch.com/blog
Templermt59@gmail.com
301-877-7746